A CATLAND COMPANION

A Catland Companion

Classic cats by Louis Wain
and many others

JOHN SILVESTER & ANNE MOBBS

MICHAEL O'MARA BOOKS
LIMITED

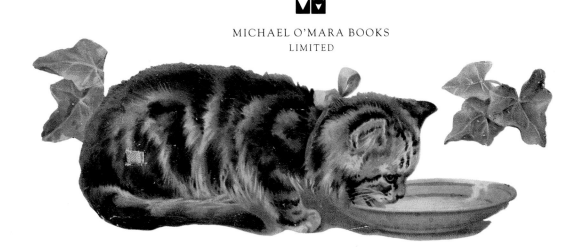

First published in Great Britain in 1991 by
Michael O'Mara Books Limited, 9 Lion Yard,
Tremadoc Road, London SW4 7NQ

Reprinted 1994

Illustrations copyright © 1991 by
Michael O'Mara Books Limited
Text copyright © 1991 by
John Silvester and Anne Mobbs

A CIP catalogue record for this book is available
from the British Library

ISBN 1-85479-765-4

Typeset by Florencetype Ltd, Kewstoke, Avon
Printed and bound in Hong Kong by
Paramount Printing Group Limited

Contents

Introduction

CATLAND existed for no more than forty years, between approximately 1880 and 1920. During those years, a wealth of colourful printed ephemera was produced, portraying every aspect of Catland life.

The cat has been closely associated with mankind for over five thousand years, and has been both worshipped as a god and vilified as an agent of the devil. The idea of Catland grew from a number of closely related events in the last century which helped to alter radically the popular perception of the cat.

In the early part of the last century, the Industrial Revolution, firstly in Europe and then in America, brought with it a great migration of people away from the land to the rapidly expanding towns and cities. The poor sanitation in the new, overcrowded urban areas quickly led to an alarming increase in the rodent population and city dwellers soon discovered that owning a cat was the best method of dealing with these pests, for cats proved to be excellent rat-catchers if not fed too often. The close, crowded conditions of town life suited them, and they enjoyed a more favoured lifestyle than hitherto. In addition to their use as rat-catchers, cats proved to be excellent pets, as they were clean and tidy, could be very affectionate, and mixed happily with children – all of which appealed to Victorian values.

Cats breeding among themselves produced many strains of attractive kittens, and the deliberate breeding of cats began to be a recognized pastime. Cat clubs and cat shows became fashionable and in 1887 the National Cat Club was formed to enable both the well-to-do and the poor to enjoy the 'Cat Fancy'.

In the early years of the Industrial Revolution, children were viewed purely as a cheap labour force, but gradually their lot began to improve. Many countries considered

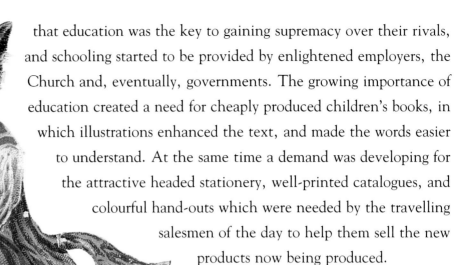

that education was the key to gaining supremacy over their rivals, and schooling started to be provided by enlightened employers, the Church and, eventually, governments. The growing importance of education created a need for cheaply produced children's books, in which illustrations enhanced the text, and made the words easier to understand. At the same time a demand was developing for the attractive headed stationery, well-printed catalogues, and colourful hand-outs which were needed by the travelling salesmen of the day to help them sell the new products now being produced.

The specialized skills of typesetters, graphic artists and lithographers were thus in great demand, and many from the continent of Europe made the trip to England or America to set up their own businesses in competition with the existing concerns which could not keep up with modern requirements.

Such publishers were initially able to draw on designs from the Continent, but when it came to cat illustrations these were very inferior. The animals depicted resembled dogs with cats' heads, for the subtlety of a cat's movement and the unique patterns of its fur were missing. Their facial expressions were inclined to be fierce, with protruding teeth and pointed ears. These Continental designs were used as plates in children's books, or more commonly for 'scraps', a new educational aid and collecting craze. Whole sheets of scraps devoted to cats are rare: they were normally shown with dogs, monkeys and other animals, or with articles of household use. Exceptions to this were a few attractive scraps of natural cats, cat heads with hats, and cats' bands and orchestras.

Meanwhile, in England during the nineteenth century, animal paintings underwent a move towards absolute realism, with the features of animal bone and muscle structures, and hair and fur patterns becoming of paramount importance. Among the well-known and admired animal artists of the day was Henriette

Ronner, who changed once and for all the way cats were portrayed. Her style of painting was to show cats and kittens together with household articles or items from the boudoir with the kittens playing and stretching and sometimes standing on two legs as they do in reality. It was probably this which inspired the whole anthropomorphic idea of cats acting out human activities.

Henriette Ronner never resorted to this device, but her 'chocolate box' studies were used by the publishers Messrs Hildersheimer and Faulkner from 1869 to 1882. Her contemporary, Horatio Couldrey, also produced similar designs for Hildersheimer and won a £50 prize in their competition in 1881 for his design of kittens in a lady's hat. George C. Witney of New York co-operated with Hildersheimer in publishing Couldrey's cat designs as Christmas card booklets.

If Henriette Ronner produced pretty but realistic studies of cats, it was left to Helena J. Maguire to raise the cats onto two legs and introduce an element of Victorian whimsy to their antics. Helena Maguire never dressed her cats, but gave them colourful bows to wear. Within a very short space of time, Maguire cats were cycling, performing circus turns, and even mixing the Christmas pudding.

Helena Maguire also worked for Hildersheimer and Faulkner in 1880 and 1881, and then joined the publishers Raphael Tuck and Sons in 1886, working with them until 1890. Her enchanting and playful designs graced countless greetings cards and calendars during this time. Later on, in the early years of the new century, her designs were used again and again on the ever-increasing numbers of picture postcards which were in vogue.

Raphael Tuck and Sons were also the publishers of the most famous

exponent of Catland illustrations, Louis Wain. It was Louis Wain in collaboration with Raphael Tuck who first coined the term 'Catland'. Although Wain never became an artist of great significance, he must be considered as a prolific and highly competent cartoonist, as well as the 'father' of Catland.

Louis Wain was the product of a narrow-minded Victorian family and as with many of his contemporaries, a strict upbringing gave way in later life to a child-like sense of humour. Unfortunately the joy and pleasure which he gave to others masked his own tragic life. Although he would have liked a career in music, Wain quickly discovered that he did not have the necessary dedication, and he therefore ventured into the world of art. He was taken on as an assistant master at the West London School of Art, but in 1880 his father died, leaving him as the sole provider of the family, and thus forcing him to find an artistic job which was more profitable.

His marriage in 1884 was disapproved of by his family, a situation made harder by the discovery that his wife was suffering from an incurable illness and so became bedridden. Their one shared joy was a black and white kitten named 'Peter' which Wain began to make drawings of. Soon his artistic skills started to receive attention, and in 1886 he was asked to illustrate a children's book entitled *Madame Tabby's Establishment*. After his wife's death in 1887, Louis Wain made friends with many artists who were later to become household names in the postcard world, and who no doubt tempted Wain to work for this medium. Due to his interest in cats, he was invited in 1890 to become President of the National Cat Club following the resignation of its Founder President Harrison Weir. It was also in 1890 that the 'Wain' cat was born, as he had begun to explore the possibilities of the comical cat, and although he hankered after producing accurate scientific cat studies, there was always a comical cat ready to jump out.

In 1896 Louis Wain collaborated with the publisher Ernest Nister to provide illustrations for a book titled *Comical Customers at our fine New Store of Comical Rhymes and Pictures*. This book was Louis Wain's first venture into the world of children's make-believe, and although his contribution was small, he clearly enjoyed his task. Included in this book are illustrations by W. Foster and G.H. Thompson, who contributed much to the animal styles which Nister made his own. Louis Wain collaborated with Nister again in 1898, when a new book, *Jingles, Jokes and Funny Folks* was produced.

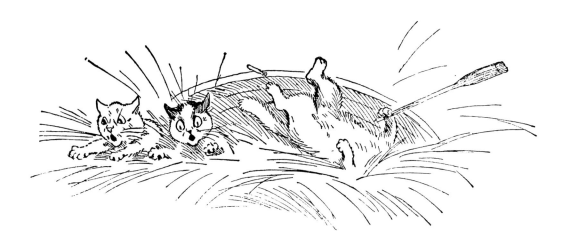

In 1902 Wain began his association with Raphael Tuck, the first book produced being *Pa Cats, Ma Cats and their Kittens*. By now, the word 'Catland' was being used, and the flow of Louis Wain material continued in the following years. The peak year for the production of Wain illustrated children's books was 1903. In the meantime, a new venture was well in hand, one which would bring Catland to a wider adult following.

This new venture was the picture postcard, which, although first produced in 1870, was only now gaining ground due to the fact that, from 1902 onwards, the picture could completely cover one side of the card. Within hours of the Postal authorities agreeing to this, the new postcards began to appear, and the latest collecting craze had started. Thousands upon thousands of designs were produced, sold and collected. The peak years of postcard sales were between 1904 and 1910, and everyone wanted Louis Wain postcards on their sales lists. He obliged wherever possible, but publishers who already had originals of his work transferred them to the new medium anyway, with or without his consent. Major publishers of the day such as Faulkner, Tuck, Valentines, Wrench, Hartmann, Davidson and Nister all produced Louis Wain cards, and his image of Catland reached millions of homes, in many lands. Sadly, Wain had failed to retain any reproduction rights in his work, and so despite his huge popularity he never received more than a fraction of what could have been owed to him.

Louis Wain was by no means the only artist associated with Catland. Other artists such as Arthur Thiele and Maurice Boulanger were closely associated with the Catland story, and in many cases produced better studies of anthropomorphic cats than Louis Wain. As well as these named artists, there were countless others who did not sign their designs, and we will never know who they were.

It is interesting to note that Louis Wain cats often sported hats, stiff collars, jackets, trousers and frocks, but hardly ever wore shoes. The exceptions to this were 'Puss in Boots', and those cats who were associated with Jackson's Hats and Boots advertisements. On the other hand, Arthur Thiele usually depicted fully dressed cats complete with boots and shoes included. There was obviously a dichotomy of opinion as to how far the anthropomorphic idea had to be followed.

By the start of World War I, the postcard boom was on the decline, and children's and nursery books were beginning to lose the charm and innocence of the Edwardian Age due to the changing social climate. From 1917 the cats of Catland were overtaken in the affections of cat lovers by the animated Felix the Cat, who was shortly followed firstly by a very famous mouse, and then by the partnership of Tom and Jerry, whose antics were rather less sedate than those of the usually genteel cats of Catland.

ACKNOWLEDGMENTS

The writers of this book wish to acknowledge the inventiveness and humour of artists such as Maurice Boulanger, Reg Carter, A. Ellam, W. Foster, A.E. Kennedy, Helena Maguire, Violet Roberts, G.H. Thompson, A. Thiele, and last, but by no means least, Louis William Wain. In addition there are also the numerous artists who did not sign their work but nevertheless have made important contributions to this book. It must not be forgotten that all these artists' efforts might have been in vain if it had not been for the expertise and skill of publishers and printers such as Davidson Brothers, C.W. Faulkner, W. Hagelberg, E. Nister, Photochrom, Raphael Tuck, Theo Stroefer, K.F. Editeurs, Max Ettlinger, Millar and Lang etc, who produced such a high standard of work so many years ago.

Apologies must be given to the late Clifton Bingham and H.M. Burnside as it will be noticed that many of the captions to the illustrations in this book bear a resemblance to the rhyming couplets that these two sentiment writers produced in never-ending supply during the Catland era.

Snowtime Cats

LOOKING at the illustrations of Catland, it would seem that January always began with cold, frosty days and deep snowfalls. Somewhat at variance with real life, where cats do not generally like the snow, the inhabitants of Catland were always shown enjoying themselves in the numerous snow scenes their artists depicted.

Heed the advice
'Danger! Thin ice'
The cats of this Nister greetings card are clearly enjoying the fun of the frozen pond. This was a theme used many times by a number of artists, but the danger of thin ice was always apparent.
c. 1900.

Sledging and ice-skating were always popular, and when the snow was deep enough kittens would build snowmen, or even perhaps snowcats, at which to throw their snowballs.

Most artists of the day liked to show cats skating in happy groups, but Louis Wain would very often depict the perils of ignoring the sign 'Danger! Thin ice'.

Spectacles, scarf, and a
funny hat
Are just the thing for a smart
snowcat

A snowman, built by the
kittens, is the subject of this
postcard by Arthur Thiele,
published by Theo Stroefer of
Nuremberg. This artist was
one of the more prolific cat
illustrators in the early
twentieth century. c. 1906.

Too late, the ice was thin
Poor young Tommy has
fallen in

A Louis Wain study of a cat
having fallen through the ice,
or perhaps, rushing forward
through a sheet of paper – it is
impossible to tell which.
Published by Raphael Tuck
and Sons in their 'Write
Away' series of postcards.

Making the most of the snow
An action-packed postcard of cats throwing snowballs by Maurice Boulanger. Published by K.F. Editeurs, Paris, *c.* 1904.

I wish I had not got rid of my horse and carriage
The open car of the Edwardian era was the butt of much postcard wit. It was certainly not a suitable means of transport on a snowy day as cars possessed no means of heating, and it was necessary to have rugs, coats and motoring hats even for the shortest of journeys.

Just cats with umbrellas
This greetings card shows cats
walking with umbrellas – a
collectable piece of Edwardian
whimsy.

Let's slip and slide
On a fast sledge ride
A snow study by Helena
Maguire showing cats
sledging. This illustration was
first used as a greetings card,
and then as a postcard.
c. 1891.

*A present
from Thomas*

An attractive cat study by the artist Violet Roberts, *c.* 1912. This artist produced a number of cards during World War I showing cats in uniform. It is said that many of her designs were first sent to her brother in the trenches for his approval. Published by Photochrom Co. Ltd.

*Come snow or shine,
This skirt's divine*

The outrageous hobble skirts and large feathered hats of the Edwardian period were often made fun of in postcards. The lady of fashion shown here is the artwork of Reg Carter, more often known as 'the Southwold Artist'.

Practice makes purr-fect

These skating cats are one from a set of twelve, depicting the months of the year. The artist is Maurice Boulanger and the postcards were originally published in France. A number were later reproduced in Tuck's 'Humorous' series. *c.* 1906.

For my secret love
Once Valentine greetings cards became popular, many interesting designs were produced, including this cute-cat cut-out of 1919, complete with red and white moveable fan.

20

Valentine Cats

THE association of St Valentine's Day with the month of February is age-old. In Victorian times, gifts of flowers, fans and bouquets were proffered and demurely accepted as tokens of affection. With the advent of sentimental greetings cards, which might be sent instead of gifts, studies of cats and kittens incorporated in designs of flowers, gloves or hearts became very popular.

Artists portrayed cats in romantic situations as well as showing that their serenading from the rooftops was not always appreciated by the human population. As a consequence of the romantic overtures of St Valentine's Day, weddings could well be expected later in the year, and these were of course illustrated in delightful greetings cards and, later, postcards.

A *Valentine Day music box*
What more likeable card for St Valentine's Day than a fold-out greetings card box, inside which is a musical cat. In Edwardian times, when the card was on sale, no music would come forth. Things are different in the microchip order of today.

A pair of star-cross'd lovers
These cards of so-called star-crossed lovers are a pair of mechanical cards published by Ernest Nister. Both illustrations are by Louis Wain. *c.* 1904.

Wilt thou be gone?
It is not yet near morn

An unusual postcard from the 'Feline Shakespeare Post Card Series', showing the famous balcony scene from *Romeo and Juliet*.

A quiet moment together
This is an unusual fan-shaped greetings card, with an illustration of two young cats by G.F. Lydon.

Musical Cats

Enough to make a dog laugh
A very attractive interpretation of the old nursery rhyme 'Hey! Diddle, Diddle!' produced by Ernest Nister, and used for book illustrations, greetings cards and postcards. A mechanical version also exists in which the cow jumps over the moon. *c.* 1898.

IN Victorian times, nearly all entertainment was live, for there were as yet few gramophone records and no radios. The talents of street entertainers provided amusement for the masses, while the concert artist, the opera singer, and the symphony orchestra provided for the few. Dancing ranged from simple social gatherings to grand balls at the fashionable houses of the day.

Balls, dances and all kinds of musical evenings were well portrayed by Catland artists, who were particularly good at illustrating those awkward situations peculiar to these occasions, such as the uninvited guest or the discordant singer.

Catland's critics enjoy the show
Whether it is the opurra, theatre, or even the circus,
these Catland critics are clearly enjoying the show.

If mewsic be the food of love
An Arthur Thiele card first published in Nuremberg, and
later used by Raphael Tuck for his 'Mewsical Cats' series.

The fiddler and his dancing class
The frenetic fiddler in this
Ernest Nister book illustration
would certainly keep his class
of kittens on their paws, as
they struggle to master the
latest dance craze rhythms
arriving from America.

A sad refrain
An illustration taken from an
early un-divided back postcard
of Continental origin,
c. 1899. This lonely minstrel
cat is clearly playing a moving
melody for his lost love.

A cat-chy tune
The cat illustrated in this
cameo is clearly playing a
lively tune on his flute. Taken
from an Ernest Nister book
print or greetings card.
c. 1898.

The band with a peculiar tone
Cat scraps were always popular, although the number of designs was somewhat limited. One successful design was that of the Catland band, in which cats were depicted playing various musical instruments. Here is just a selection of the band for your enjoyment.

The prima ballerina

Cats are by nature graceful animals, and their movements are often ballet-like, even if they are only stretching in front of the fire. Here is a greetings card published by Wolff Hagelberg.

The leading tenor

A cat study by Arthur Thiele which appears to depict 'the leading tenor' of the Opurra House, who just happens to have his music with him.

A happy Christmas.

The ball
A greetings card from the
1880s showing cats with other
animals. The rhyme on the
reverse side of the card states
'Pug meets Puss with greetings
hearty.' The cats shown are
the thin and fierce ones, so
typical of early Catland
illustrations.

The prima donna returns
Like opera singers in real life,
Catland's prima donnas are
always willing to make a
come-back, and sing a number
of their favourite arias.

The Opurra Box
The well-to-do in Edwardian times would often own an 'opurra box', where it was fashionable to be seen. An illustration taken from an embossed greetings card.
c. 1895.

Kitten on the keys
This illustration is from a greetings card produced by Ernest Nister, an outstanding publisher of quality books, greetings cards and postcards. The initials G.H.T. appear on many of the animal illustrations he used.
This artist was in fact G.H. Thompson, and the style of this illustration is very much his. *c.* 1898.

Dignity and Impudence
This rather 'snooty-puss' is
clearly not amused by the
younger cat wearing this year's
fashions. She herself is still
wearing those of last year,
which are quite good enough.

Haute Cature

APRIL in Catland always brought the promise of spring, and its inhabitants, although not shedding their fur coats, were always as keen to wear the latest fashions as their human counterparts. Eastertime, with its fashion parades, often occurred in April, and cats in new bonnets and hats were everywhere.

Edwardian artists frequently used the medium of the picture postcard to make fun of the outrageous fashions of the day – the large hats and hobble skirts – many of which can be seen here. Sometimes, very daringly for the period, female cats were even portrayed smoking cigarettes in public.

Footloose and fancy-free
Mr Thomas is having his shoes shined, prior to meeting his latest lady love, who is anxiously awaiting his arrival. The shoeshine illustration is from an Ernest Nister greetings card. The lady cat card is in the style of Maurice Boulanger, but is not signed.

Almost a lady

This lady seems to have dressed somewhat hurriedly, and although she has obviously seen better days, she appears to have forgotten them on this occasion. Illustration from a French postcard, artist unknown, but in the style of Maurice Boulanger.

Feathers bright, and flowers so gay
It is the gentlecat who has to pay

These three illustrations are all by Arthur Thiele. They show the expense of dressing fashionably, as feathers and imitation flowers were never cheap, a fact well known to the male cat looking on, and waiting no doubt to pay the bill. Cards published by Theo Stroefer, Nuremberg. *c.* 1906.

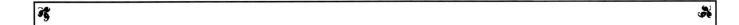

The bad girl of the family sees another beau

The 'bad girl of the family' is in this case depicted by Violet Roberts. Clearly, the cat in question has broken all the social rules of the day. Not only is she smoking in public, she is also prepared to dress daringly and flirt with everyone. Just look at the number of broken-hearted admirers she has discarded.

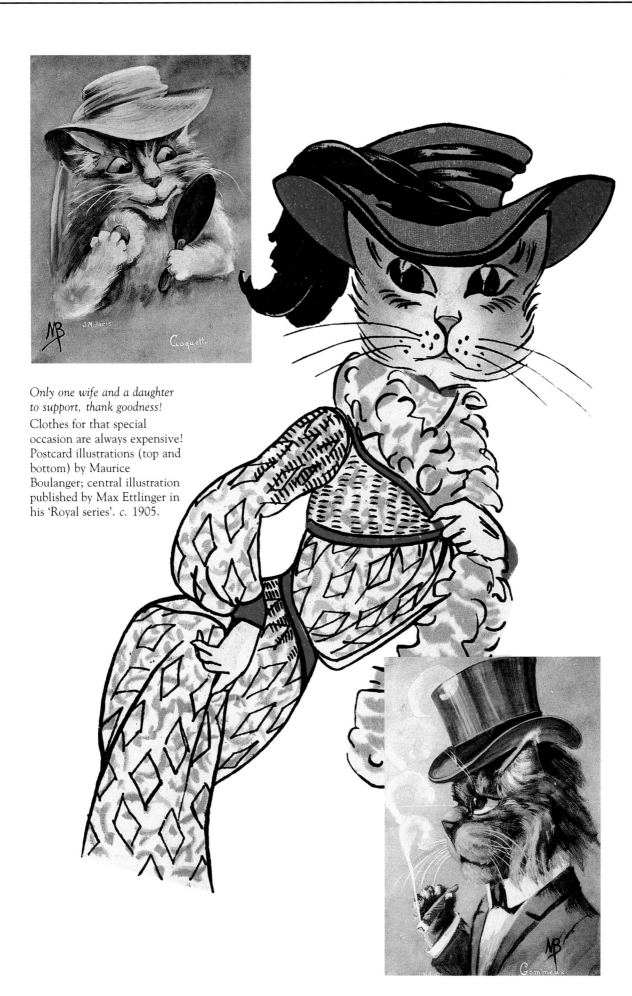

Only one wife and a daughter to support, thank goodness!

Clothes for that special occasion are always expensive! Postcard illustrations (top and bottom) by Maurice Boulanger; central illustration published by Max Ettlinger in his 'Royal series'. *c.* 1905.

'Mashed' –
With bonnet so bright,
I wonder whom she
will meet to-night
A 'masher' was an
Edwardian term meaning a
man-about-town, who would
flirt with any female gullible
enough to fall for his
attentions.   The illustration
is from a Raphael Tuck
salesman's advertising card.
The salesman would show this
to various buyers, and quote
the prices for items required.
The item here is a large
brightly illustrated scrap.

I wonder if this is really suitable
The cat shown on this
delightful scrap is clearly
unsure as to whether she has
bought the right materials.

RAPHAEL TUCK & SONS. LONDON.

"MASHED."

SIXPENCE THE SHEET.

Cats at School

As the majority of Catland books were written for children, scenes of the school classroom were popular. Catland artists showed good kittens being rewarded, while lazy and dull kittens were made to wear the comical dunce's cap which at one time was kept in many schools.

Kittens of all kinds in Catland abound
Catland illustrations often portrayed the pleasures of school life. Here are two examples of how this was done. The dunce is from a Louis Wain Calendar for 1917 whilst the charming little greetings card is of some twenty years earlier.

The subjects taught in Catland schools were very similar to those in real life, with reading, writing and arithmetic for the younger kittens and history, geography and science for the older ones. Bird- and fish-keeping were more specialized subjects.

The principal school in Catland was undoubtedly Dame Tabitha's Academy. Like other schools of the period, its standards were assessed at regular intervals by the school inspector, whose visit made the month of May not so merry for those who failed his tests.

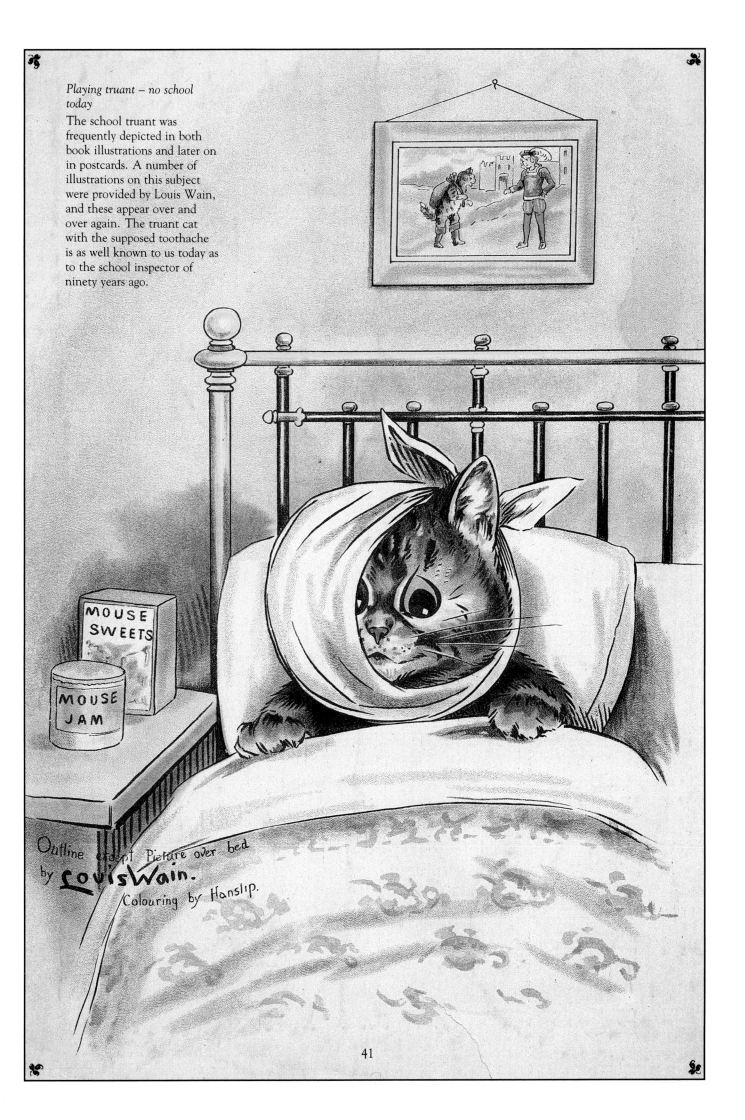

Playing truant – no school today

The school truant was frequently depicted in both book illustrations and later on in postcards. A number of illustrations on this subject were provided by Louis Wain, and these appear over and over again. The truant cat with the supposed toothache is as well known to us today as to the school inspector of ninety years ago.

MOUSE SWEETS

MOUSE JAM

Outline except Picture over bed by **Louis Wain**. Colouring by Hanslip.

Whatever can this be?
School scenes were a subject often illustrated on scraps, and small cameos of cats with slates, with jars and cages, or with globes were always popular.

How do you spell 'cat'?

'Can't spell "cat"? Disgraceful! Why I could spell it with only three mistakes long before I was your age!'

This illustration, supposedly of Dame Tabitha's Academy, is probably the best known of all Louis Wain's schoolroom studies. Parts of it were later used for a series of postcards; greetings cards were also produced from it. The illustration probably first appeared as a two page spread in *Pa Cats, Ma Cats and their Kittens* published by Raphael Tuck and Sons in 1902.

See if you can find Catland

I have invited Mr Rat to visit us today
Arthur Thiele also liked school subjects for his series of
postcards. Shown here is the school biology class which
Mr Rat was invited to attend. He declined to stay for tea
however, as might be expected.

I think it should be knit one, purr-l one
In this classroom study by Arthur Thiele, the school
inspector seems to have found some flaws in the knitting
produced by Miss Purr's class. A postcard first published
by Theo Stroefer of Nuremberg, and later by
C.W. Faulkner and Co. in England.

Two naughty kittens, in trouble again
One stays in, whilst the other risks the cane

The kitten 'staying in' after school is from a postcard illustration by G.H. Thompson, published by Ernest Nister *c.* 1904. The slate for writing and copying was a standard item of school equipment.

The other naughty kitten being admonished by his teacher is taken from a stand-up greetings card. The style is very much that of Louis Wain.

Sporting Cats

In June, when the Catland days were sunny and warm, the summer sports of cricket and tennis began in earnest. Football was also played, although the season had officially ended. A new sporting craze in Edwardian times was that of cycling, and the roads of Catland were often filled with teams of racing cyclists wearing bright caps and blazers. Accidents occurred frequently, but as the roads were still relatively free of motor cars no one really got hurt. Another popular sport portrayed by Catland artists was that of golf, with the players resplendent in their plus-fours and tam-o'-shanters.

As with summers everywhere, the weather could turn wet, and then cats would be forced to go indoors to play table tennis or billiards.

I think you've hit a birdie
Postcard illustration by Millar and Lang in their 'National' series.

Don't hit the caddy, hit the ball
Although golf has long been a popular sport, it has not always commanded the professionalism and the large sums of money which it attracts today. In this book illustration by Louis Wain, we see the simple golfer of the olden days about to 'drive'. The plus-fours, gaiters, and tammies of the illustration are no longer commonly seen.

My *service, I believe*
This attractive cameo is taken
from a pull-out calendar for
1907, published by Raphael
Tuck, in which several sports
are depicted. Tennis was
always a popular Catland
subject, with Louis Wain's
'One to Love' probably the
best known illustration.

I say, anyone for tennis?
Fashions may have changed
but the typically English
phrase 'Anyone for tennis?' is
known the world over. This
illustration is taken from a set
of six postcards showing
various sportsmen of the time.
c. 1909.

Tally Ho!

One of the most popular Edwardian sports was that of cycling. The roads were as yet almost devoid of other mechanical transport, so the horse and carriage, or the horse-drawn coach, were the chief hazards to the cyclist.

The lone rider

Many types of bicycle were developed, the ultimate design being that of the 'safety bicycle', which was very similar to that of today. The lady in blue is riding a cycle of this type, and looks set to scare off horses from her path if need be.

A bicycle made for two

The popularity of the bicycle was firmly enshrined in the popular song of the music hall – 'A Bicycle made for Two'. The cycle in question was most likely the tandem, but other bicycles for two were equally popular.
c. 1880.

A motor accident in Catland

This accident scene is from a postcard by Maurice Boulanger, from a series titled 'In Catland' published by Henry Moss and Co. *c.* 1904.

The cause of it all

Rounding the corner with the greatest of speed,
The skating cat took little heed.
The motor car travelling fast
Could neither stop, nor squeeze past.
The resultant accident had to be seen to be believed.

Kitties tub race
A book illustration by Louis Wain in which kittens are using washing tubs as boats.

Paddling to adventure
A small greetings card published by Ernest Nister shows cats in a canoe, a somewhat unusual design.

Waiting for a cat-ch
An oft-portrayed scene by
Louis Wain, in which all that
the cats appear to have caught
is an old boot. This design
was used as a book
illustration, a greetings card,
and a postcard and is still
being reproduced today.
*c.*1903.

I am the champion
A Christmas greetings card
which folds back to stand up.
The illustration is by Louis
Wain, and the card is from
the Diadem Series published
by the innovative company of
Wolff Hagelberg.

Diabolo: even Baby plays it
One of the crazes of the
Edwardian era was 'Diabolo',
an ingenious toy in which an
hour-glass-shaped top was held
on a string and spun. The idea
for the game is said to have
been brought to Europe from
China by missionaries. In
1906 a Frenchman, Gustave
Phillipart, made it popular in
France. Both Louis Wain
(as here) and Arthur Thiele
produced postcard sets
depicting the craze.

51

*Penny-farthings off at a pace
I wonder which cat will win the
race*
This illustration is taken from
a greetings card published
c. 1885 by J.T. Schipper. The
bicycles shown here are all of
the penny-farthing type,
which as can be seen, were far
from safe.

Three wheeling
After the more famous bicycle
for two of song fame, came
the tricycle for two. Either
cats or people could sit side by
side in comfort and safety. No
back-seat driver here! Book
print *c.* 1880.

Cyclists beware!
An attractive motoring cameo
from the 1907 Raphael Tuck
calendar, in which Pa and Ma
Cat have taken to using the
latest means of transport. The
cars were depicted in a very
stylized manner, as was
common at the time.

The chance of a catch
One of Catland's summer sports was cricket, and this Louis Wain illustration of a rather attacking field is to be found on a postcard advertising Jackson's hats and boots. The cats depicted are fully dressed in 'whites' and of course cricket boots. *c.* 1911.

Paws before wicket
This scene is the third to be taken from the Raphael Tuck 1907 Calendar, and shows that dreaded moment when the cry is 'paws before wicket', an upsetting time for any batsman.

Seaside Cats

DURING the month of July, every inhabitant of Catland who was able to, went on holiday. If the artists of the day are to be believed, the seaside was especially popular, for in Catland the sky was always blue, the sun hot and the beaches golden-brown.

The seaside resorts of Catland always provided plenty of amusements.

We all like to be beside the seaside
A delightful family group out for a walk along the Promenade. Visiting the seaside, even for a day trip, was becoming fashionable in Victorian times, and everyone had to look their best. Greetings card published by Ernest Nister. *c.* 1898.

Most kittens were eager to go for a swim from the row of brightly painted bathing huts at the water's edge, while rowing boats were always popular, providing the sea was calm. For the less adventurous, there were deck chairs to laze in and sand-castles to build. Minstrel shows were a feature of the seaside, and no beach would be complete without an old sea cat telling tales of his days on the pilchard boats in far-away oceans.

I say, have you seen the mew-sic man?

No Victorian or Edwardian beach would have been complete without its share of entertainers: jugglers, magicians, singers and minstrels. The latter would give their renditions of the popular songs of the day. Book print published by Ernest Nister. *c.* 1898.

Round and round the kitties go . . .
Fairgrounds were always popular, especially at the seaside. The new steam-driven roundabouts, complete with tuneful organs and whistles, were particularly thrilling. Book print published by Ernest Nister. *c.* 1898.

Are there shrimps for tea?
With rock pools as yet
unpolluted by twentieth-
century progress, it was easy
to net your own shrimp tea.
Postcard by Maurice
Boulanger, published by
Henry Moss and Co. *c.* 1904.

Kitty's first dip
Sea bathing was a popular
Victorian pursuit, and even
the youngest members of the
family would be persuaded to
enter the water. Book print by
G.H. Thompson, published
by Ernest Nister. *c.* 1898.

The Sea Mew sails round the bay
Three trips each day
A stand-up calendar opening out to a boat shape. Published by Raphael Tuck and Sons in 1910.

Giving the girls a treat
A typical 'saucy puss' postcard
which would have been on
the postcard racks in *c.* 1910.
The artist Violet Roberts
produced a number of sets of
postcards on the holiday
theme. Published by
Photochrom Co. Ltd in their
'Celesque' series.

Don't watch the birdie
This attractive greetings card
illustration dates from 1889,
and is very much in the style
of Helena Maguire, although
unsigned.

The sun is shining, the sea is blue
Soon there'll be no room for you
This scene by Louis Wain shows the typical bathing machines of the day, used for undressing in before entering the sea. Postcard published by Valentines 1908.

The sea cat's tale
No seaside harbour would have been complete without its collection of old sea cats and fishermen, telling tales of distant shores.

Cross your paw with silver
Seaside resorts also attracted fortune tellers from far distant places who would be looking for a gullible holidaymaker with money to spare.

The yachtsman needs an off-shore breeze

What a luxury, breakfast in bed

A novel event was to have breakfast in bed, normally charged as an extra. The cats depicted here are by the artist A. Ellam and are from a series of postcards on this theme. Publisher Raphael Tuck and Sons. *c.* 1912.

I hope we can afford to come again

The worst part of any holiday was the bill for the lodgings, and it could be difficult to 'raise the wind' to pay it, as the Edwardians used to say. On this postcard by Louis Wain, published by Wrench Ltd in 1905, the bill indicated is unbelievable for the period.

Famous Cats

WHILE everyone enjoyed the sun, sea and sand, Pa Cat tried to relax in his deck chair and quietly read the newspapers. In August, there was not much news to tell and the papers had to resort once more to describing the exploits of those two famous cats of Catland, Puss in Boots and Dick Whittington's cat. More sensational newspapers ran stories about Jack and his magic beanstalk – but could they really be true?

The famous pair
Catland's most famous citizens were Puss in Boots, and the cat belonging to Dick Whittington. Here are just two small reminders of these well-known stories. One is from a scrap, the other from an advertisement hand-out.

Jack the Giant-Killer
Louis Wain revealed that Catland possessed many more famous felines. A look at the prints, drawings and postcards produced by this artist show that nearly all the well-known fairy-tale characters were in fact cats. Illustration from a book print or postcard published by Raphael Tuck in their 'Christmas Series'. *c.* 1905.

Puss tries on his hat and gloves
The story of the miller's third son who inherited only a cat from his father, is often recounted in Catland. Puss, you may remember, requested an expensive pair of boots, a hat, and a pair of gloves, for he knew that if dressed in the right clothes he would be taken for the servant of a very important master.

Puss on his master's business
Louis Wain portrayed Puss in Boots telling all those at work in the fields to say they were working for the Marquis of Carabas. The King believed the tale, and noted that these were fine fields, whose owner would be a fit suitor for the Princess's hand in marriage.

Puss dreams of riches

While trying on his boots, Puss was scheming
how he could persuade the King that his master
was indeed the important Marquis of Carabas.
By guile, he killed the ogre in the castle, just in
time for the arrival of the King and the Princess.
Like all fairy tales it has a happy ending, as you
may have already guessed.

The thieves are caught
Another illustration by Louis Wain from Raphael Tuck's 'Christmas Series'. *c.* 1905.

Dick Whittington's cat nears London

The story of Dick Whittington is world famous. The poor boy decided to come to London to seek his fortune. He brought with him his pet cat, but when they arrived in London, the streets were not paved with gold as he had been told. He started to return home, but heard the bells of London calling him back, whilst his cat was already walking in that direction. On this occasion he found work with a City merchant, and after several adventures in which his cat helped him, he was promoted and eventually married the merchant's daughter. He became a successful merchant, and then Lord Mayor of London.

Pa Cat misses a clean sweep
No Edwardian home would have been considered neat and
tidy unless it had had its weekly 'going over'. While this was
going on Pa Cat would retire either to his office or his club.
Illustration by Arthur Thiele for a postcard series. *c.* 1906.

It must be fine, the washing's on the line
Before the advent of the washing machine, the Monday
wash was a heavy chore, which depended on a bright breezy
day to dry the clothes. Illustration by Arthur Thiele for a
postcard series. *c.* 1906.

Domestic Cats

By September most of the inhabitants of Catland had returned home. Mother Cat was keen to catch up on her household chores and so as soon as she started dusting and beating curtains and carpets, Pa Cat quickly escaped to work.

Later in the day, after all the work had been done, Pa Cat would appear for tea with all the family, in true Edwardian tradition.

As in real life, many Catland families were able to afford servants and a nanny whose job it was to look after the kittens, and take them for a walk in the park each afternoon. At the weekends, the whole family might be seen taking the air, with Pa Cat in striped blazer and boater accompanying Ma Cat and the kittens in their pram.

Safe and sound,
We're homeward bound
Although railways provided a means of mass transportation in the Victorian era, they are depicted on very few Catland illustrations. Here is just one example, taken from a greetings card. The style is that of Helena Maguire, but the drawing is unsigned.
c. 1895.

Tea time in the nursery
Postcard published by Ernest Nister. *c.* 1903.

Father's trying to read the paper
This illustration, often titled 'Cats At Home', shows Pa Cat trying to read his newspaper. Kittens were to be seen and not heard.

The tabby twins in chairs so high
Have dropped the bowl, and spoilt their pie
The twins illustrated are taken from part of the front cover of the nursery book, *Pa Cats, Ma Cats and their Kittens* published by Raphael Tuck and Sons in 1902.

A well-deserved cat-nap
When the day's chores were
completed, what better time
to have a well-earned cat-nap,
even if it might be disturbed
by the quarrelling of fractious
kittens.

*The roast will soon be done to
a turn*
This charming cameo is
taken from a greetings card
published by Sockl and
Nathan, who made use of a
number of cat designs from
the Continent. The thin and
fierce-looking cats are very
typical of early cat art. This
illustration shows to
advantage the old-fashioned
means of cooking. *c.* 1885.

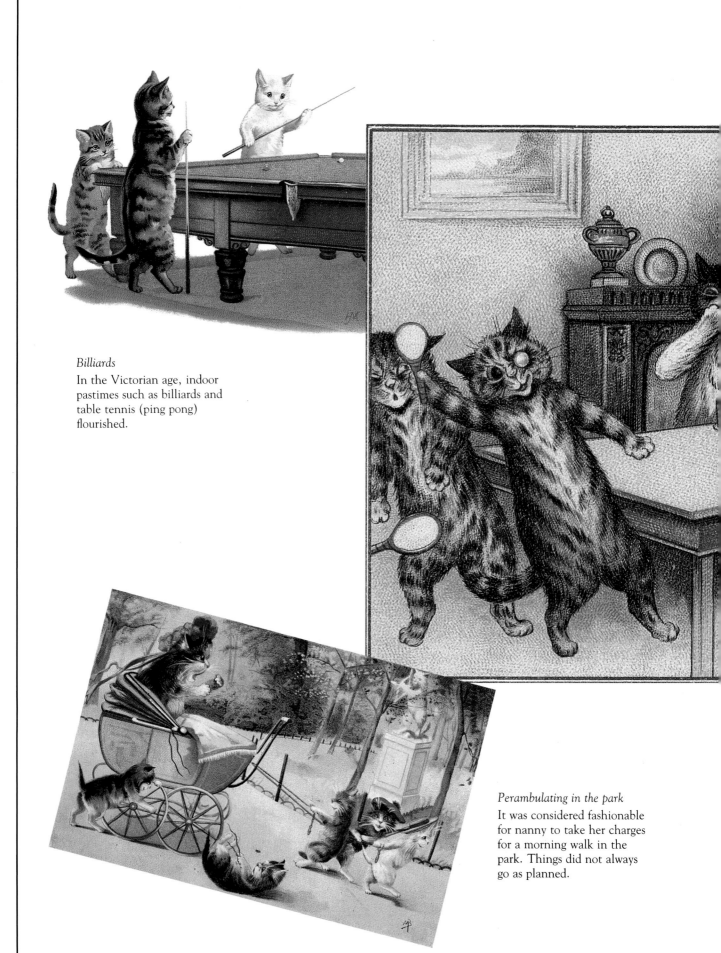

Billiards
In the Victorian age, indoor pastimes such as billiards and table tennis (ping pong) flourished.

Perambulating in the park
It was considered fashionable for nanny to take her charges for a morning walk in the park. Things did not always go as planned.

Ping Pong
The beauty of billiards and ping pong was that they could be easily pursued during inclement weather. No fashionable country house weekend would have been considered complete without them.

Playing hoops
Hoops and sticks were inexpensive toys of the period, and no kitten would have wished to be without one. Never seen today, this toy needed much skill to master properly.

Cats' cradle
At the end of the day kittens would be put to bed, in this instance a very fancy Victorian cradle. Ma Cat is happily dozing by the fire. A Louis Wain illustration, published by Raphael Tuck and Sons in their 'Art' series. *c.* 1903.

Poor Aunt Jane,
I hope she'll soon be well again

A popular subject for greetings cards. The illustration here is in the style of Helena Maguire.

Rub and scrub
The washing in the tub

Another illustration by Arthur Thiele for a postcard series. *c.* 1906.

Kittens at the table waiting for their tea,
There's mouse creams and rat pie for everyone to see.
A tea-time scene by Louis Wain.

Tea-time tantrums
This illustration is taken from an aquatint published by
Theo Stroefer of Nuremberg. The work dates from *c.*
1898 and is typical of the early style of cat illustrations
originating on the Continent.

'O you naughty kittens!
Whatever have you done?'
'We are playing cat's cradle
And having lots of fun.'
The age-old game of cat's
cradle is shown here, taken
from an illustration by
William Foster who did much
work for the publisher Ernest
Nister. Often his illustrations
were not signed. Here,
however, is a clear example of
his work. Illustrations such as
this were used as book
illustrations, greeting cards
and postcards. *c.* 1900.

Proud of their mittens
This illustration by A.E.
Kennedy is taken from a set of
six picture postcards which
tell the story of the kittens
who lost their mittens.
A.E. Kennedy worked on
many children's books for
the publishers Blackie and
C.W. Faulkner. *c.* 1920.

79

A young witch
This illustration is part of an advertising card for Eagle Brand Condensed Milk, hence the inclusion of the kittens.

Pumpkin surprise
Hollowed-out pumpkins, with eye holes and cut out mouths, were very much part of Hallowe'en. They were placed behind windows, with lighted candles inside them, presenting an eerie sight at night-time. This illustration is taken from a Hallowe'en greetings postcard by the artist Ellen Clapsaddle, perhaps better known for her children's studies.

Hallowe'en Cats

IN October the cats of Catland prepared for Hallowe'en by hollowing out pumpkins and collecting apples for apple bobbing. Hallowe'en was not taken too seriously in Catland, however, for in the legends of witches associated with Hallowe'en, cats are considered evil. This light-hearted treatment can be seen in the work of American artists such as Ellen Clapsaddle who was very popular in the Edwardian period, producing many thousands of postcard designs.

Don't worry I'm not scared. It isn't real, you know
These cats are really scared, although they pretend not to be. An illustration by Louis Wain.

Apple bobbing and a lucky black cat
At Hallowe'en parties (more an American event than English) the game of apple bobbing is popular. Just for good luck we have included a black cat.

Ghostly visions
This is a Louis Wain scene set late on Hallowe'en evening, when there appear to be a good number of ghostly dancing cat shapes on the lawn. A book illustration.

Five for a penny
The cheapest of any
As well as the recognized shops, the streets of a Victorian town would have had many street-side stalls or markets. Many large companies of today started in this humble fashion. Illustration taken from a greetings card. *c.* 1895.

Soon be home
Even the most careful of cats could sometimes lose their kittens in the fray of going shopping. Fortunately in Edwardian times there was often a friendly policeman to come to the rescue, and return the missing offspring safely home. A postcard illustration.

I saw it first
The age-old battle of shopping, especially at sales time, is well depicted here by Louis Wain. An illustration taken from a set of six postcards published by E. Wrench Ltd. *c.* 1905.

Shopping Cats

DURING the dark days of November, Catland's cats could be found busy shopping in preparation for Christmas. Well-lit shop windows were full of games, toys and other presents, while inside the shops the familiar crush developed around the bargains. In such a crowd, it was easy for Ma and Pa Cat and their kittens to be separated.

When everyone had more than enough parcels to carry, the long walk home had to be made, cheered by chestnuts from the hot-chestnut seller.

Guess who is going to be first at the sales
A dedicated shopper, undoubtedly on her way to the sales, does not even have time to notice the hot chestnut seller and his brazier. This cat was certainly going to get any bargains going. Illustration from a scrap.

A farthing change, please

Most items for sale, especially in Edwardian drapers' shops, were priced down to the level of the smallest coin – the farthing. Assistants would often be slow in giving this change, as it could be a perk. A keen-eyed shopper as depicted by Louis Wain would not be taken in, however. Postcard published by Davidson Brothers. *c.* 1904.

Kitty Jane is so very vain

A charming illustration by G.H. Thompson for a Nister postcard published in *c.* 1904.

Ladies, you will still find fur trimmings are very popular
A keen Edwardian shop assistant would always give friendly advice (even if not asked) to his customers. This was especially true of lines that were not selling too well. The illustration here is a typical Ernest Nister item, used in books, and on both greetings cards and postcards published by the firm.
c. 1900.

If you haven't got a penny, a half-penny will do
A delightful illustration of kittens at the village shop, first used as the cover for the nursery book, *Comical Customers at our Fine New Store of Comical Rhymes and Pictures*, published by Ernest Nister in 1896. Later on the design was used for an advertising postcard for Charnley's Biscuits.

Pa Cat, Ma Cat, and Kitten too,
Are going shopping to see what's new
This illustration is taken from the Maurice Boulanger set of twelve postcards depicting the months of the year. First published in France it was re-issued by Raphael Tuck in their 'Humorous' series, appropriately titled 'Shopping'.

Well-heeled pussies
Any collector of cat ephemera will quickly discover that cat and kitten illustrations were used extensively in Victorian and Edwardian advertising. They were not only depicted on items of a feminine nature, but were used to advertise stores, agricultural machinery and patent medicines. Here is a delightful shoe cut-out dating from 1883, on which Mr D.F. Cowles's latest selection of wallpapers, decorations and drapes were listed on the back.

Christmas Cats

THE majority of Catland illustrations on greetings cards and postcards depict scenes associated with the festivals of Christmas and the New Year. The Catland Christmas was a traditional Christmas, with Christmas stockings, a Christmas pudding decorated with holly, and a visit to the pantomime or circus.

One artist in particular who glamorized this time of year was Helena Maguire. Her work in the 1880s and 1890s produced the groups of tabby cats and black cats which are still appearing on cards today. While Helena Maguire showed the preparations for Christmas, it was Louis Wain who produced many of the Father Christmas cat designs and Maurice Boulanger who showed kittens hanging up their stockings and dreaming about their presents.

Christmas gifts
A fold-out greetings card of a cornucopia of presents, with cats looking on.

Party time
Small talk seems to be in progress during the party, if this Louis Wain greetings card is to be believed. Screens, palms, fans and bows all add to the Edwardian atmosphere.

The Christmas tree, so merry and bright
Gives cats and kittens great delight

It was not very often that a Christmas tree was depicted on Christmas greetings cards, so this illustration is somewhat unusual. The be-ribboned cat is almost certainly by Helena Maguire. The tree decorations are very typical of the period. *c.*1895.

Santa arrives with gifts for all
One of a number of Louis Wain Santa Claus illustrations, reproduced from a greetings card. The word 'Yuletide' was frequently used instead of 'Christmas', as on this card. *c.* 1908.

Pleasant dreams and present hopes . . .

An imaginative postcard by Maurice Boulanger, in which the cat asleep dreams of the presents he would like. In fact, the small vignettes are actually taken from other postcard illustrations. *c.* 1905. In the other illustration, the cats are hanging up their stockings and leaving their boots by the fireplaces for the arrival of Santa overnight.

. . . are sometimes to-morrow's disappointments

It looks as though Grandma Cat has received the wrong presents. She asked for knitting wool, and got a doll, a ball and some marbles by mistake. A Louis Wain greetings card published by Raphael Tuck and Sons.

92

Here comes the pudding plump and round.
Did your wish come true?
The artist of this small greetings card is not known, but it was published by S. Hildersheimer and Co. c. 1895. This firm was responsible for many attractive items, but its artists were never acknowledged.

Stir the pudding and make a wish
The making of the Christmas pudding and its arrival at the dinner table was frequently depicted on seasonal greetings cards. The artists never seemed to be sure whether the pudding should be round or basin-shaped. Helena Maguire produced many of the designs that we know of. c. 1900.

The Christmas circus – what a treat!
As Catland artistes perform their feat

A large number of greetings cards and postcards were produced showing cat circus acts such as jugglers, tumblers, tight-rope-walking cats, and trapeze cats. Many of the designs appear similar to the work of Helena Maguire, but there are slight differences of style. The majority of these cards were of Continental origin, and many are now being reproduced once more as greetings cards.

Wallflowers

In 1905 Louis Wain produced six designs for Raphael Tuck's 'Humorous' series. Two of the designs showed male and female 'wallflower' cats. What a pity the two cards did not get together, and the cats meet each other.

Louis Wain.

Purr-fect Balance

This is an embossed greetings
postcard showing a snowcat
instead of a snowman. An
unusual variation on the very
large number of postcards
showing cats in snow scenes.
c. 1904.

A year-long tale we now have penned
And so at last we reach the end.